MARBLES!

History, Secrets and
The Worlds Best Marble Games!

Written by
Matthew Hawkins

Illustrations by
Monitor Graphics

Mud Puddle Books
NEW YORK

This edition published in 2006 by
Mud Puddle Books, Inc.
54 W. 21st Street
Suite 601
New York, NY 10010 USA

info@mudpuddlebooks.com

Originally published by
Hinkler Books Pty Ltd
17 – 23 Redwood Drive
Dingley Victoria 3172 Australia
www.hinklerbooks.com

© Hinkler Books Pty Ltd 2004

Written by Matthew Hawkins
Illustrations by Monitor Graphics

ISBN: 1-59412-133-8

© Hinkler Books Pty Ltd 2003

Printed and bound in China.

Contents

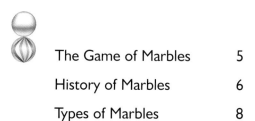

The Game of Marbles   5

History of Marbles   6

Types of Marbles   8

Marbles Lingo   10

Shooting   14

Marbles Games

Lagging   16

Lagout   17

Bossout   18

Saucers   19

Ring Taw   20

Bounce-eye   22

Pots and Pans	24
Bridgeboard	26
Hundreds	28
Road Runner	30
Bull's-eye	31
Dobblers	32
Rocky Road	34
Tic-Tac-Toe	35
Pyramids	36
Pyramid Dice	37
Pyramid Madness	38
Marble Siege	40
Rolley-hole	42
Marble Billiards	44
Marble Golf	46
Index	48

The Game of Marbles

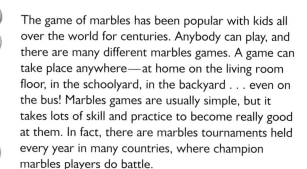

The game of marbles has been popular with kids all over the world for centuries. Anybody can play, and there are many different marbles games. A game can take place anywhere—at home on the living room floor, in the schoolyard, in the backyard . . . even on the bus! Marbles games are usually simple, but it takes lots of skill and practice to become really good at them. In fact, there are marbles tournaments held every year in many countries, where champion marbles players do battle.

This book will teach you the tricks and skills every good marbles player needs to know. You can learn the names of each kind of marble and how valuable they are. You can also learn the special words marbles experts use when they play the games. We'll show you how to shoot marbles, from the simplest methods to ones that need more practice. And there are twenty different marbles games that you and your friends can play, from Bridgeboard and Road Runner to Marble Siege and Marble Billiards.

Before long, your marbles will be streaking left, right and center!

History of Marbles

Marbles is a very old game. The earliest marbles ever found are five thousand years old! They were discovered in Egypt, buried with a child. Marbles that are almost four thousand years old have also been found on the island of Crete (near Greece). The American Indians have been playing marbles for centuries.

Children of the ancient Roman Empire used marbles made from sea-rounded pebbles, fruit pits, and nuts. The game itself was called 'nuts' and was played by children during the festival of Saturnalia, held in mid-winter. And what were the rules of 'nuts'? Nobody knows! The rules of the game have not survived.

The earliest known word for 'marbles' is French: 'bille', meaning 'little ball'. This word first appeared over eight hundred years ago. The game was

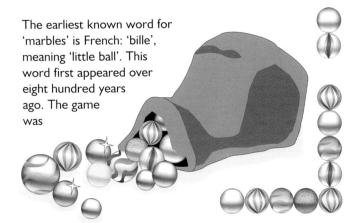

called 'bowls' and 'knikkers' until 1694, when the balls were first made out of marble stone and imported from Germany. Then the name 'marbles' was adopted.

Marbles reached its greatest popularity in the USA in the 1920s. The US National Marbles Tournament of 1923 was held in Washington DC, and included players from all over the country. The final attracted 5000 people and contestants were treated like celebrities wherever they went. The winner was fourteen-year-old Harlin McCoy. Although the tournament still exists, it is not nearly as well-known as it was. However, it still has a small group of loyal fans, who pass their interest on to new generations.

Types of Marbles

Marbles come in all shapes, sizes and colors, and are made from many different materials. Some are highly prized—especially 'lucky' marbles (those which have won many games).

An 'alley' is the best kind of marble. These are made from a soft, whitish stone called alabaster, or other semi-precious stones. Alleys are always large, and because of their value can be traded for handfuls of lesser marbles.

Ordinary glass, stone and clay marbles are less prized. Glass marbles are the most common and have many names, depending on their appearance. They may be called 'cat's eyes', 'glassies', 'rainbows' or 'swirls'. Sometimes, ball bearings or steel balls are used as marbles, and these are called 'steelies'. The marbles used to shoot with, usually lesser marbles, are called 'taws' or 'shooters'.

The colors in common glass marbles are added when the glass is still soft and hot. The glass is cut into cubes, and then the cubes are ground into spherical marble shapes by rollers. Finally, the marbles are polished.

Because your marbles are very valuable to you, decide before beginning your game whether you are playing for 'keeps' or not. It is a great marbles tradition to play to win other people's marbles, but just as much fun can be had if you return the marbles to their owners after the game is over.

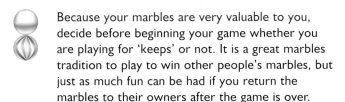

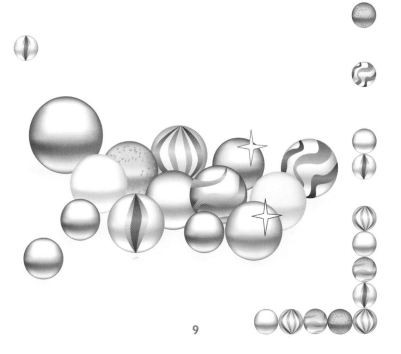

Marbles Lingo

Impress your friends with your knowledge of marbles by learning these words!

AGGIES: Shooters made from the mineral agate (a hard kind of stone). The term has also come to mean marbles in general.

ANTE: The equal number of marbles each player begins a game with.

ALLIES: Prized shooters made from semi-precious stones. The name comes from the word *alabaster*, which is the stone allies are often made from.

BOMB: To drop a marble from shoulder height, with the aim of scattering a cluster of marbles below.

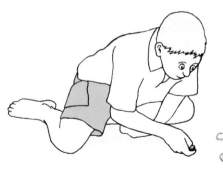

BUMBOOZERS: Large marbles.

CAPTURE: To win another player's marble.

CAT'S EYES: Glass marbles with distinctive bands running through them that make them resemble the eyes of a cat.

CHALKIES: Unglazed marbles made from clay or limestone.

CLEARIES: Clear glass marbles in a variety of single colors.

DUBS: When two or more marbles are knocked out with one shot.

FAT: Used to describe a shooter that you have lost, and is trapped inside the game.

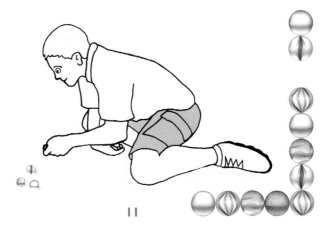

GLASSIES: Marbles made from glass, either clear or colored.

IMMIES: Glass marbles that are streaked with color so that they resemble aggies. Immie is short for 'imitation'.

JACK: A direct hit on another player's marble.

KNUCKLING DOWN: The shooting technique used by marbles experts.

MIBS: The game of marbles, from a shortening of the word 'marbles'.

MIBSTER: A marbles player.

MILKIES: White, opaque marbles.

PEE WEES: Small marbles.

RAINBOWS: Marbles with many colors.

SHOOTER: The marble used to aim at a target or strike other marbles in a game.

STEELIES: Marbles made from steel, often a ball bearing. They can be either solid or hollow.

STONIES: Ordinary brown marbles made from stone or clay.

SWIRLS: Glass marbles with bands of color running through them from top to bottom.

TAW: Another name for a shooter, but usually a name given to a prized or lucky shooter.

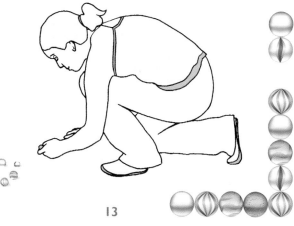

Shooting

Shooting is the most important skill for a marbles player. The more accurate you are, and the harder you can shoot your marble, the more marbles you will win. There are three ways that marbles are usually shot, and you can practice and perfect each.

Rolling

Rolling is recommended for beginners and younger children. It will help get you started in learning how to shoot marbles. First, eye your target up and check whether there is any slope to the playing surface (rolling works best on perfectly flat surfaces). Then roll the marble along the ground as you would any other ball. With luck, you'll hit your target! Rolling is very easy to do, but can be both inaccurate and slow.

Flicking

Flicking requires a little more practice than rolling, but you will make more winning shots with this move. Put the marble on the

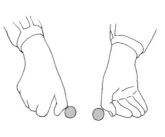

ground and then put the tip of your thumb on the ground behind it. Smoothly flick the marble away with your forefinger. This method produces a very fast shot but because it can be inaccurate, it is best used only for very close targets.

Knuckling Down

You will need lots of practice to get this one right, but it's worth the effort. This is the method champion marbles players use. Resting your knuckles on the ground, place your

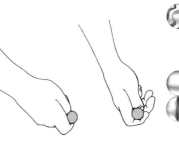

shooter in the crook of your forefinger. Then rest your thumb behind the shooter. Smoothly flick the shooter away with your thumb. When this is done well, it makes for a very fast, very accurate shot.

Lagging

This is a very simple game that can be used instead of a coin toss to determine who goes first in a game. It's one of the first marbles games most people learn, and is a quick way to get a more complicated game started when you become an expert at marbles!

1. Draw a line on the ground. You can also play this game up against a wall.

2. Players shoot marbles from 3 feet (about 1 meter) away or more, towards the line or the wall. The aim is to get as close to the line or wall as possible, without going over the line or hitting the wall.

3. The player closest to the line or wall wins.

Lagout

This is an excellent game for beginners and can be played alone, or with other people. It's a good game to play if you want to practice your marbles skills when none of your friends are around. You will need a flat surface near a smooth wall to play.

(1) Players throw a marble at the wall, so that it rebounds and lands somewhere in the playing area.

(2) The aim is to rebound your marble off the wall so that it hits a previously thrown marble, without bouncing first. If you do this, you win all the marbles on the ground and the game starts again.

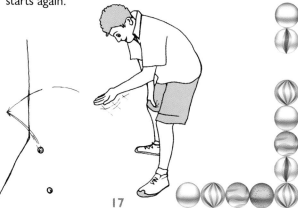

Bossout

Here's a good game with which to practice your shooting. It's simple, quick and lots of fun. Bossout also makes a great warm-up game.

(1) Draw a shooting line on the ground with chalk (if you are outside), or lay a piece of string along the floor.

(2) From the shooting line, Player One bowls a marble to any distance. This is the target marble.

(3) Player Two shoots a marble at the target marble. If Player Two's marble comes to rest within a span of the target (a span is the distance between your outstretched thumb and forefinger), or they get a 'jack' (a direct hit), they win the target marble. If their shooter does not reach within a span of the target, it is collected by Player One.

Saucers

Here's another game that is lots of fun and will help improve your shooting. You will need a shooting line and an old coffee saucer. Make sure the saucer is an old one, just in case it breaks during the game!

(1) Lay the saucer on the ground about 5 feet (1.5 meters) from the shooting line.

(2) From the shooting line, Player One shoots their taw at the saucer. If they miss the saucer, the marble stays where it is. If they hit it, they collect a marble from Player Two, and can have another try.

(3) The first player to hit the saucer five times in a row wins all of the marbles that have missed the target, and they win the game.

TIP
As your shooting improves, move the saucer further and further away from the shooting line, to make it harder for yourself and improve your accuracy.

Ring Taw

This is the most popular marbles game. It is played all around the world and there are many variations of it. Here is one of the most common.

1. You will need to draw a circle on the ground if you are outside. If playing indoors, draw a circle on a large piece of paper. The circle should be about 10 inches (51 centimeters) across. Make sure the circle is about 6½ feet (2 meters) from your shooting line.

2. Each player puts the same amount of marbles in the ring (usually five), clustered in the center. They bowl in turn from the shooting line, and the player whose marble is closest to the circle's edge gets to start.

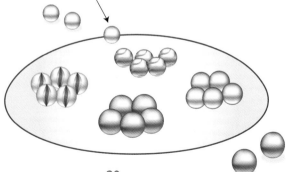

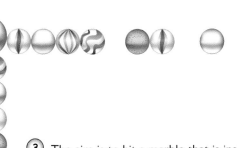

3 The aim is to hit a marble that is inside the ring, knocking both it and your shooter out of the ring. If you manage to do this, you keep both marbles and get another turn. If your taw stays inside the ring, it is 'fat' and must stay there. If you knock any marble out of the circle, you win it. If you are good enough, you can knock out more than one marble.

4 When the ring is empty, the player with the most marbles is the winner!

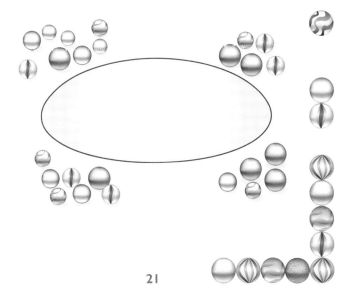

Bounce-eye

The aim of this exciting game is to 'bomb' as many marbles out of the ring as possible. Several players can join in—the more, the merrier!

(1) Draw a circle on the ground, 12 inches (30 centimeters) across.

(2) Each player puts an equal number of marbles in the center of the circle. Marbles of different sizes should be used—say, two large marbles and three small ones for each player.

22

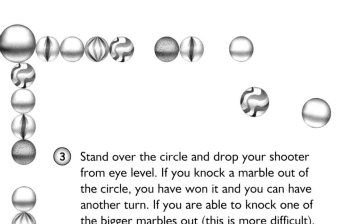

(3) Stand over the circle and drop your shooter from eye level. If you knock a marble out of the circle, you have won it and you can have another turn. If you are able to knock one of the bigger marbles out (this is more difficult), you can use the big marble as the shooter on your next turn.

(4) The player with the most marbles when the circle is empty is the winner.

TIP

It's best to drop your marble carefully into the ring, rather than throw it down hard. You will then be more accurate.

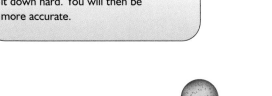

Pots and Pans

This is a very loud game, so don't play it in the classroom! You will need five pots and pans of different shapes and sizes. Old frying pans are good, and stove pots and flowerpots can be easily found. The aim is to throw your marble into the air so that it lands in a pot or a pan.

(1) Line up the pots and pans about 6½ feet (2 meters) from the shooting line. They need to be numbered from one to five. The biggest pot should be number one, and the smallest

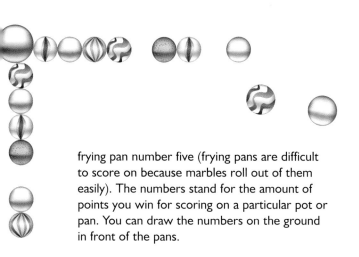

frying pan number five (frying pans are difficult to score on because marbles roll out of them easily). The numbers stand for the amount of points you win for scoring on a particular pot or pan. You can draw the numbers on the ground in front of the pans.

(2) Players take it in turns to throw for a pot or a pan. Your throwing hand cannot go beyond the shooting line. If it does, you forfeit your turn.

(3) If your marble lands in a pot or pan and stays inside, you win the number of points for that pot or pan, and you can have another turn. If you bomb a marble that is lying on the ground, you score ten points and another turn. Keep your score on a sheet of paper.

(4) The player with the most points after five rounds wins the game.

Bridgeboard

This is a very old game that is fun to play with a large group. It also requires accurate shooting, so brush up on your skills before playing!

(1) Before the game, you need to build your bridge. Find a big cardboard box and cut some holes along the bottom of the box, for the marbles to pass through. Cut the holes in sizes ranging from very small to very large. Then number the holes from one to five, with number one as the largest hole, number two as the next largest, and so on. If you want to make your bridge stand out, cover it in bright wrapping paper, or paint it.

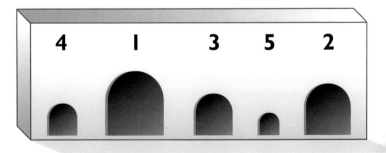

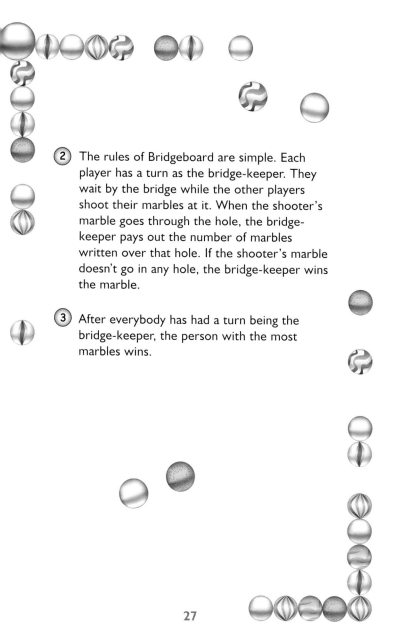

(2) The rules of Bridgeboard are simple. Each player has a turn as the bridge-keeper. They wait by the bridge while the other players shoot their marbles at it. When the shooter's marble goes through the hole, the bridge-keeper pays out the number of marbles written over that hole. If the shooter's marble doesn't go in any hole, the bridge-keeper wins the marble.

(3) After everybody has had a turn being the bridge-keeper, the person with the most marbles wins.

Hundreds

The aim of Hundreds is to score one hundred points. The game is played between two people and is very exciting to watch when expert players are playing. You will need a pen and paper to keep score.

(1) Place a small cardboard box on the ground about 6½ feet (2 meters) from the shooting line.

(2) The players have to shoot a marble into the box's opening. If both marbles go in, it is a draw, and nobody scores. If Player One gets theirs in but Player Two misses, Player One scores ten points.

28

3. If both miss, the player whose marble is closest to the box has another chance to shoot. They can choose to aim for the box (any part of it), or the other player's marble. If they hit the box they get five points, and if they hit the other player's marble they get twenty points.

4. Whoever gets to one hundred first shoots for the game. If they get the marble in, they win the game. If they miss, the other player gets ten points. If they both reach one hundred, they have a shootout—the best of three shots.

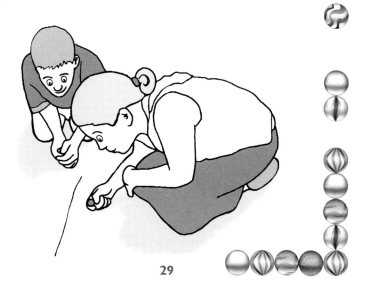

Road Runner

*This game of skill and accuracy comes from Peru.
You will need to play it outside, on a long, flat
surface. A pathway is best—don't use a real road!*

(1) Draw your 'road' first. It needs to be about 12 inches
(30 centimeters) wide, and at least 16½ feet (5 meters)
long. At the far end of the road, draw a finish line.

(2) Player One rolls a marble as far along the road as
possible without going out of bounds. If their marble
goes out of bounds, they are out of the game.

(3) Each successive player tries to hit a marble that is
lying on the road. If they knock another
player's marble off the road, that
player is out of the game.

(4) The first player to reach the finish
line, or the last player left standing,
is the winner.

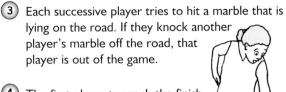

Bull's-eye

This game is a little like darts. Games of Bull's-eye can last for a long time, depending on the number of players. It's best played in a group of three or more. You will need a pen and paper to keep score.

(1) Draw four circles on the ground, or on a sheet of paper. The smallest circle should be about the size of a saucer. Number them as shown.

(2) Each player takes three shots from the shooting line. The score is added up from where the marbles lie in the rings. The next player can knock the other player's marbles out of the rings, and if they do, the other player loses 5 points.

(3) The first player to reach 150 points has to try for a bull's-eye. If they miss, they have to wait their turn again. The first player to get to 150 points and then get a bull's-eye is the winner.

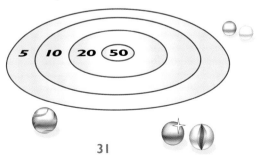

Dobblers

This game is easy to play, so it's great for times when a group of beginners and more experienced players are playing together. The aim is to score as many 'jacks' as possible.

(1) Each player puts three marbles on a line opposite the shooting line, at a distance of 3 feet (about 1 meter) from it. Make sure there is a gap of about 4 inches (10 centimeters) between each marble.

(2) Players take turns shooting at the marbles from the shooting line. If you score a direct hit, you win the marble and your shooter back, and you can have another turn. If you miss, you lose your turn and you have to take your next shot from where your shooter ended up. If another player hits your shooter, you have to add a marble to the line.

(3) When no marbles are left on the line, the player with the most marbles is the winner.

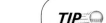

TIP
More experienced players can be given a handicap in this game, and stand further back from the shooting line. This will give beginner players a better chance!

33

Rocky Road

Ever seen a champion golfer lining up for a putt? Here's a game that will test how well you can "read" the footpath.

(1) Choose a rough footpath with cracks running along it.

(2) Player One places their marble somewhere on the path, within 6½ feet (about 2 meters) of the shooting line, and in a place where it will be hard to hit. Then they offer a prize of five marbles for whoever can hit it.

(3) If a player misses the target marble, they forfeit their shooter to Player One. If they hit the marble, they win five marbles from Player One.

(4) After everybody has had a turn offering the prize, the player with the most marbles wins.

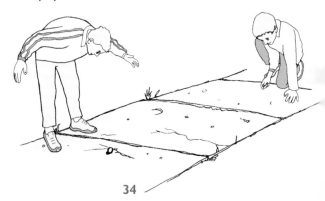

Tic-Tac-Toe

*Tic-Tac-Toe isn't a marbles game, right? Wrong!
This quick, simple game is fun for everyone.*

(1) In order to tell the marbles apart, each player should
have half-a-dozen in a different color than his/her
opponent's. Draw a tic-tac-toe board on the ground,
or on a sheet of paper 6½ feet (about 2 meters) from
your shooting line. It can be any size.

(2) Toss a coin or lag to decide who goes first. Players
have to shoot their marbles into the squares. You can
knock your opponent's marble out of the square they
are in. If you miss the board completely you can have
another turn, until you get your marble on the board.

(3) The first player to
get a line of three
of their marbles
across the board,
horizontally or
diagonally, is the
winner.

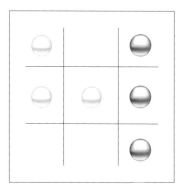

Pyramids

This is a popular game that has been enjoyed around the world for many years. If you play it well, you're sure to win lots of new marbles!

(1) Each player kneels an equal distance apart, and builds a pyramid of marbles on the ground or floor: three on the bottom as a base, and one on top. You can also play this game with a base of nine marbles (three by three in a square), topped by four marbles, and one on top.

(2) Players take it in turns to shoot at the next player's pyramid. If you knock down a pyramid, you win the pyramid plus your shooter. If you miss, the pyramid-owner keeps your shooter.

Side View

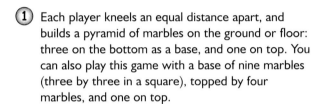

Top View

36

Pyramid Dice

This game is an exciting variation of Pyramids and it involves chance, as well as shooting skills. You will need some dice for this game—one for each player.

(1) Each player builds a pyramid base of three marbles and places their dice on the top, with the number one facing upwards.

(2) Players take it in turns to shoot down each other's pyramids. If they knock down a pyramid, the number facing upwards on the dice when it lands is the amount of marbles the pyramid-keeper has to pay that player. If they miss, the pyramid-keeper wins the shooter.

Side View

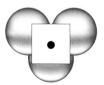

Top View

TIP

Try playing Pyramid Dice with larger pyramids, as with the regular game of Pyramids. Players don't win or lose any more marbles when smaller pyramids are built, but it's lots of fun!

Pyramid
Madness

Go crazy and build the largest marble pyramid you can! If you have lots of marbles, you can attempt to build a pyramid of stupendous size. If you don't have enough marbles, you can build a pyramid with your friends, pooling your marble resources.

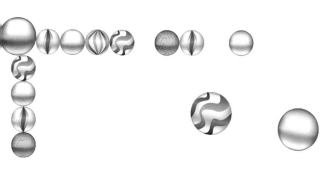

1 It's best to build your pyramid on flat lawn or on carpet, so your marbles don't roll away. Start with eight by eight marbles as your base, and build upwards from there.

2 Once you've mastered a pyramid with a base of eight by eight marbles, increase it. Try ten by ten, or twenty by twenty. Before you know it, you'll need a step-ladder to reach the top. And watch out for low-flying aircraft!

TIP
Pyramid madness is best played with a large group of friends. You could hold competitions— form teams of two or more, with each team pooling their marble resources. The winning team could win a set number of marbles from other players.

Marble Siege

Can you capture the fortress of marbles? Each player will need at least eleven marbles for this exciting game—and good shooting skills are essential.

(1) Draw a target on the ground, or on a large sheet of paper. The target should consist of four circles, each larger than the last. The largest circle should be 20 inches (51 centimeters) across.

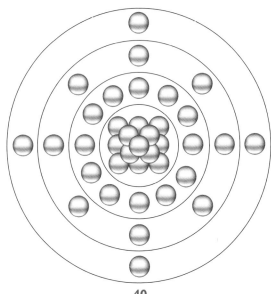

(2) Each player puts one marble in the outer circle, two in the next, three in the next, and four in the innermost circle. Put your biggest marbles in this innermost circle, and make a pyramid out of them. This is the fortress.

(3) Players take turns shooting at the outermost circle. The same rules apply as for Ring Taw: if you hit a marble out and your shooter rolls out of the circle as well, you win both and have another turn, etc.

(4) When the outermost circle is empty, players shoot for the marbles in the next circle, and so on.

(5) The pyramid of marbles in the innermost circle has to be 'bombed' out, using the same rules as Bounce-eye. Once this circle is empty, the player with the most marbles wins.

Rolley-hole

This traditional marbles game is played along the Kentucky-Tennessee border in the United States of America. The version here has been simplified, as the tournament version is very complex. Each player uses only one marble. You will need a large, flat area to play this one, and it is the most fun when played outside on a sunny afternoon.

(1) Traditionally, three evenly-spaced holes are dug in a line down the center of the yard. The best substitute is to use six boxes, taped together back to back, and laid on any flat surface.

Team One

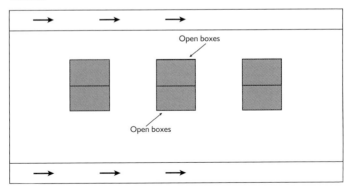

Team Two

Overhead view of Rolley-hole playing area

(2) Each team is made up of two players. There is a coin toss to decide who goes first. The winner of the coin toss moves up the field, until they are opposite the first open box. They roll their shooter at the opening, followed by an opposing team member, who is moving along the opposite lane. The third player to roll is the partner of the coin toss winner, and they shoot from wherever their partner was up to.

(3) If you get the marble in the box you take another turn, moving up the field to the next box. The aim is to score twelve times, moving up and down the field. Once you have scored, you have 'made' that box, and it is safe. That is, you have one down and eleven to go. If you miss completely, your partner has to try and make that box on their next turn.

(4) Moving up and down the yard, the first team to make twelve successive boxes wins the game.

Marble Billiards

This popular indoor game requires great skill. It is best played on a large rectangular rug, or on carpet marked out with string into roughly the size of a pool table. It is played with two teams of two players each.

1. Each player will need a chopstick. This is what you will shoot your taw with, in the same way you would use a pool cue. It's a lot trickier than it seems!

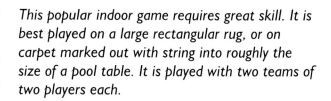

2. Place twenty-four marbles at one end of the rug, in a triangular shape, (see below). Included in the twenty-four should be one large marble from each

44

of the two teams. These are the 'master' marbles, and count for three points each. The other, smaller marbles are worth only one point each. Stick three small paper labels onto the rug at the other end. You can shoot from any of these.

(3) A coin is tossed to decide who gets the 'break'. The winning team shoots their marble from one of the three spots, and tries to hit the cluster of marbles and break them apart. The aim is to knock as many marbles as possible off the edge of the rug. If the first player knocks off a marble and their shooter stays on the rug, they get another turn. If their shooter rolls off the edge of the rug, any marbles they knocked off are 'spotted', that is, put back in their original spot, and the next player gets two shots. If they fail to hit any marble, they also forfeit two shots.

(4) When the rug is clear of marbles, the team with the most points wins the game.

Marble Golf

You've heard of mini-golf? Well, marble golf is just as fun. A word of warning—check with an adult first that it's okay to dig a few small holes in the garden. An alternative to digging holes is to place old saucers at the site of the holes. This will save the lawn and keep everyone happy!

(1) First, dig nine small holes in the ground, on a flat grassy lawn. Don't make the holes too deep—they should be just deep enough for the marble to roll in and stay there. Think carefully about your course design. The holes could be placed in a square, round or S-shape around the lawn. Alternatively, place nine old saucers about the lawn. Number the holes from one to nine. You'll need a pencil and paper for scoring, too.

(2) Start the game from a starting line, a short distance from the first hole. The aim of this game is to make your way around the course with the least number of shots, as with regular golf. Before the game, arrange that a number of marbles from each player be given to the winner.

(3) Toss a coin to see which player goes first. The first player shoots a marble towards the first hole, and continues on until their marble is in the hole. The score is then written down and the second player takes a turn, and so on. Note: marbles must never be thrown, but shot towards the hole using one of the three shooting techniques on page eight.

(4) Total up the scores at the end of the game and see who the winner is!

Have fun!

TIP
Add exciting obstacles and traps to vary your marbles golf course. Small mounds of earth, cracks, rough spots in the ground and sticks all make the game more difficult.

Index

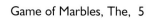

Bossout, 18
Bounce-eye, 22
Bridgeboard, 26
Bull's-eye, 31

Dobblers, 32

Game of Marbles, The, 5

History of Marbles, 6
Hundreds, 28

Lagging, 16
Lagout, 17

Marble Billiards, 44
Marble Golf, 46
Marble Siege, 40
Marbles Lingo, 10

Pots and Pans, 24
Pyramid Dice, 37
Pyramid Madness, 38
Pyramids, 36

Ring Taw, 20
Road Runner, 30
Rocky Road, 34
Rolley-hole, 42

Saucers, 19
Shooting, 14

Tic-Tac-Toe, 35
Types of Marbles, 8